ABRAHAM LINCOLN

A Life from Beginning to End

D1172982

Table of Contents

Introduction

He may have been the most reviled president in American history. As loathed in his time as much as George Washington was revered in the country's early years, Abraham Lincoln served as president at a period when the survival of the United States was very much in doubt, just as it had been when Washington took office. Although their political eras may have shared a similarity in crisis, the paths which had brought each of them to power were vastly different. George Washington, who grew up in prosperity and ascended to the aristocracy, was born with advantages which Abraham Lincoln lacked. Unlike the handsome and courtly Virginian with the elegant wife, the assurance of class, and the substance of property, the tall, homely frontiersman was described as a gorilla in opposition newspapers; his sense of humor was derided as coarse and vulgar; his wife was despised for Southern birth and for her temperament. But the two men, generally regarded as the two most successful men to serve as presidents of the United States, actually do share certain traits in common. In particular, they each relied on their own abilities to get things done. Circumstances prevented both men from obtaining the education they would have liked, but each man taught himself the skills that he needed to make his way in the world and, as fate showed, to alter the course of the world's direction.

These men, the first and sixteenth presidents of the United States, lived in times of perilous national events but neither ever lost their own moral compass. Each was conscious of their duty as captains of the ship of state and their ability to adhere to their view of their destination kept a nation on course. Both the majestic Mount Rushmore and the mundane American currency remind Americans daily that the country owes its survival to men who sacrificed physical comfort and pleasure for a cause greater than any personal crusade.

In sacrificing his life, Lincoln became a martyr for the country in which he believed so emphatically that he would not allow the United States to splinter. The American ideals which were the cornerstone of his philosophy are preserved in his prose; Lincoln, perhaps more than any other president except Thomas Jefferson, knew how to turn a phrase. Jefferson had the advantage of his College of William and Mary education; Lincoln had an affinity for words which turned his personal grief, his emotional valleys, and his sense of doomed destiny into poetry. Meet Abraham Lincoln, the president of the United States whose life was a love poem to his country.

Chapter One

Born on the Frontier

"I remember my mother's prayers and they have always followed me. They have clung to me all my life."

—Abraham Lincoln

Thomas Lincoln and his wife Nancy Hanks Lincoln had been married for almost three years when their second child, a son they named Abraham, was born near dawn on February 12, 1809. Nancy had sent Tom to fetch a midwife because her time was approaching. Neighbor Peggy Walters went to wait with Nancy while Tom was on his errand; although only 20 years old, Walters had assisted her mother in delivering other babies in the community.

Hodgenville, Kentucky was a frontier community where childbirth was a matter for the women to handle. Walters would recall years later that the Lincolns, like the others in their community, were poor but didn't lack what they needed, and that Nancy had a good feather-bed beneath her, and enough blankets. In recalling the birth, Walters remembered that Tom had been solicitous of Nancy and that his wife was glad that she'd had a son.

Future years would not offer cause to look back upon many such episodes of domestic affection in the Lincoln household. The Lincolns would not have an easy life, and while young Abraham knew hardship from the time of his birth, his knowledge of life came from the experience that had more in common with the America that he would govern than a gilded existence that other power brokers might have known.

The Lincoln Family

Tom Lincoln was born in Virginia in either 1776 or 1778. His family moved to Kentucky not long after, where his father Abraham owned over 5,000 acres of rich Kentucky land. In 1786, while they were planting corn, an Indian attack killed Abraham. An older son, Mordecai, saved Thomas before an Indian could kill him. Thomas survived, but because his father died without leaving a will, the land went to his older brother and Thomas was left to earn his living through labor as a farmer and carpenter. There was little opportunity for an education, but he was willing to work hard. He bought a farm in 1802 and married Nancy Hanks in 1806. When Abraham, named for Tom's father, was born in 1809, he was born on the new farm that Tom had purchased.

Records show that Tom Lincoln was a wage earner who was respected in his community. Yet his hard work and savings failed to lead to prosperity, as Kentucky's land title system was inconsistent and Tom could not claim the title to the farms that he'd purchased. Too often, he had to sell the land for less than he'd paid for it. Fed up with the lack of opportunity, and also opposed to slavery which was legal in Kentucky, the Lincolns moved to Indiana.

Abraham Lincoln recalled life in Perry County, which had an average of three people per square mile, as a fight with trees and logs and grubs. The land was a challenge for farmers and Tom depended on hunting to feed his family.

Their one-room cabin had no flooring and minimal furniture; the corn-husk beds upon which they slept were a favorite home for rodents and bugs.

Nancy Hanks Lincoln, unlike her husband, stressed the value of education and when a school was started nine miles from their cabin, she insisted that the Lincoln children would attend, no matter what Tom thought. Although the school didn't last, the two children attended while it was open, walking anywhere between two to three hours each way just for the opportunity.

A New Mother for the Lincoln Children

The family lost Nancy in 1818, when she died from eating contaminated milk taken from cows that had eaten poisonous white snakeroot. With young children to raise, Tom Lincoln couldn't stay a widower for long. He left eleven-year old Sally and nine-year old Abraham to manage for themselves while he returned to Kentucky to find a wife. Tom was gone about six months, leaving the children with very little to eat. A neighbor who checked on them noted that the Lincolns were thin and filthy and that the cabin was dirty.

When Tom returned in a horse-drawn wagon, he brought a widow named Sarah Bush Johnston to join the Lincoln household as his wife and stepmother to his daughter Sally and son Abraham. Sarah brought three children to the household, and Nancy Hanks' cousin Dennis Hanks also lived with them. Sarah and her stepson were immediately fond of each other; she was a loving person who was affectionate with both her own children and her stepchildren. She couldn't read, but her new husband had told her about his son's interest in books and when she came to Indiana, she brought six books for him. She also encouraged the children to attend school; one, which lasted only three months, had opened up a mile away. Lincoln's total time of formal schooling lasted less than 18 months but the fact that he had even that much is due to the women who mothered him. The new Mrs. Lincoln was also a tidy and orderly housekeeper; the cabin eventually grew to have a wooden floor, as well as a door and a window.

Lincoln, Father and Son

Father and son were emotionally distant from each other. Some historians believe that this was because Tom failed to realize how deeply the death of his mother affected Abraham. But Abraham Lincoln, as an adult, spoke disparagingly of his father and his lack of education, and there was a definite gap between the boy's intellectual yearnings and his father's willingness to nurture them. For Tom, reading was idleness and he felt that Abraham's time would have been better put to use in doing work.

Some accounts say that he hid his son's books or even destroyed them. He was also said to punish his son with a beating when he caught him reading. Tom Lincoln adhered to a rough code of parenting; when Abraham misbehaved, or corrected his father, or was disobedient, Tom's punishment was physical. However, this was not unusual for the times. Tom seemed to favor his stepson John Johnston, but Abraham remained close to his stepmother.

Tom Lincoln's stern parenting may have been the reason that his son would later be an overly indulgent father. Many years later, Lincoln's future law partner, William Herndon, would write how irritating it was when the rambunctious Lincoln boys would play in the law office, upsetting the books and the inkwells, and Lincoln did nothing to punish them or curb their behavior. Herndon wrote: *I have felt many and many a time that I wanted to wring their little necks, and yet out of respect for Lincoln, I kept my mouth shut.* Ever the fond parent, Lincoln did not note what his children were doing or had done, and would follow that same practice when he and his children were together in the White House.

Although the rift between father and son would last throughout Tom's life, Abraham did visit his family when he was a practicing lawyer, although the sentiment was for his stepmother rather than his father. But when Tom Lincoln needed money, Abraham helped him out. When Tom was dying, however, Abraham chose not to visit him, and when his father passed away in 1851, Abraham didn't attend the funeral. There was a link to his father, however; when Abraham Lincoln's wife gave birth to their fourth son, he was named Thomas. – though he would come to be known as his nickname Tad. Reporters at the time were curious about Lincoln's background, but he seldom talked about it and never mentioned his father.

When Lincoln was 17 years old, he found work on a ferryboat; he enjoyed the life on the river, and when he was 19, he built a flatboat to deliver farm produce to New Orleans. When the produce was delivered, he sold the boat for timber and returned home, giving the money he'd earned to his father; it was the accepted practice at the time, but not one that pleased the young man.

The family moved again in 1830, this time to Illinois. Lincoln was not yet 21 and he went with the family, but by the time he had turned 22, he left the family home and moved to New Salem, Illinois.

Chapter Two

Lincoln's Life in New Salem

"At New Salem, Lincoln found himself. The activities and contacts of his New Salem years revealed the possibility of betterment and gave him some conception of his own capacity."

—Benjamin Thomas

Upon arriving in New Salem, Lincoln was hired as a clerk in a general store. At six feet, four inches tall, Lincoln would have been noticed no matter what he did, but his feats as a wrestler and rail splitter impressed his new neighbors with his physical strength. His customers at the general store, which also served as a community meeting place, enjoyed Lincoln's engaging wit and humor. His literacy was useful for members of the town who couldn't read or write and needed help. New Salem was a community where for the first time, Lincoln could enjoy himself.

Lincoln's New Life

Lincoln boarded at the local tavern during his first year in town, where the tavern keeper's daughter, Ann Rutledge, was regarded as pretty, quick-witted, and kind. She was also engaged to another man; although Ann was attracted to

Lincoln, she regarded her engagement as binding and refused to renege on the agreement until she could tell her fiancé in person, as he had gone to New York on business.

But there was plenty for Lincoln to do in his new community besides fall in love. Six months after Lincoln arrived in New Salem, he declared himself as an independent candidate for a seat in the Illinois state legislature. Shortly after entering the race, he signed up for a 30-day term to fight in the Black Hawk War, which broke out in 1832. The other volunteers named him as the company's temporary captain, an honor which meant a great deal to him.

Lincoln's romance with Ann Rutledge continued to be in limbo; her fiancé had not yet returned, and although the Rutledge family now lived on a farm several miles away, Lincoln continued to visit her. Their romance was private, known only to her family. Residents of the town noticed that Lincoln visited the Rutledges often, but there was relatively little speculation regarding his reasons.

Romance was not the only thing on Lincoln's mind when he returned to New Salem after the end of the Black Hawk War. Although his political campaign failed because his military service had taken him out of the community and he wasn't able to acquaint himself with the rest of the district, he won 277 of the 300 votes cast in New Salem. However, he was a stranger to the rest of the county and as a result came in eighth out of a field of thirteen candidates. In 1835, he turned his attention to the law, studying on his own and passing the state bar exam in 1836. He began to participate in local politics and served as the secretary when the Whig Party had its meetings.

Lincoln's zeal for the law and politics may have come about not only from personal interest, but also from grief. The spring and summer of 1835 had been the hottest on record for Illinois, with rain almost daily. When the rain ceased, the weather turned hot and stayed that way from August until October. During that time, people began to fall ill, and among them was Ann Rutledge. Her family thought the illness was brain fever, but it may actually have been typhoid. The story of Lincoln's grief at her death likely would have remained a private one, but William Herndon, who would become Lincoln's friend and law partner, would later make the details public after Lincoln's death, embarrassing the widowed Mary Todd Lincoln with his assertion that Ann Rutledge was the great love of Lincoln's life.

Lincoln's Involvement in Politics

Even though he wasn't a Democrat, he was appointed the New Salem postmaster by Democratic President Andrew Jackson. But Lincoln, despite his political instincts, avoided partisan wrangling. Jackson's appointment may have had less to do with Lincoln's party affiliation and more to do with the fact that there were no Democrats in New Salem who coveted the position. The position only paid $55 a year, so Lincoln continued to earn money by chopping wood, splitting rails, working as a county surveyor, as well as doing legal work.

When he ran for the Illinois state legislature for the second time in 1834, Lincoln would prove victorious - and he had support from the Democrats as well. He conducted a minimalist campaign: no promises, no platform, and relatively few speeches. His campaigning ran on his personality, as he told stories, visited almost every family in the county, and shook hands. He continued to win in subsequent elections, voting along Whig party lines. But politics in the nation was undergoing a change as the slavery issue began to dominate. In 1837, Lincoln and five of eighty-three legislators expressed their opposition to a resolution that condemned the abolitionist movement.

Mary Todd

In 1840, Lincoln met the woman he would marry, but the romance would be star-crossed and the union stormy. Mary Todd, born in Lexington, Kentucky in 1818, was well educated and had attended a prestigious school for girls; she had told people that she intended to marry a man who would become president. Mary's ability to speak French, which she learned at Madame Charlotte LeClere Mentelle's Boarding School, was an asset in the future when she became the First Lady and was the social hostess to international guests. Her parents were wealthy and her father was socially connected to political men of influence, which inspired Mary's interest in politics. Her father, Robert Todd, had served as the Kentucky House of Representatives clerk for 20 years before he was elected himself to Congress. The Todds owned slaves, but Mary's political interest included a firm belief in the abolition of slavery.

She was 21 years old when she met Lincoln, ten years her senior. However, her parents didn't regard him as a suitable match for their daughter, as her previous suitors had included the celebrated Stephen A. Douglas. Her mother had died when Mary was seven years old and her father remarried not long after, to a daughter from a prominent Kentucky family; the couple would have more children who would, unlike their half-sister, support the Confederacy.

Mary Todd was strong-willed. The couple would become engaged despite the wishes of Mary Todd's family, yet in 1841, Lincoln called off the engagement. More than a year later, Lincoln and Mary Todd once again began seeing one another, and shortly after the renewal of their romance they were married on November 4, 1842. Both Lincoln and Mary Todd may have suffered from forms of mental illness; he may have been a victim of depression, and she may have suffered from bi-polar disorder. There was no treatment, or even diagnosis, at the time for conditions such as this; Lincoln dealt with his dark moods and preoccupation with death by telling funny stories, but Mary's temperament was different. The Civil War, which claimed so many casualties, may also have claimed the First Lady whose emotions made her fragile at a time when grief was nationally prevalent.

Whatever the future would hold, Mary Todd had the makings of a supportive political wife in Illinois. She followed her husband's career with avid interest. She gave wifely attention to his wardrobe, a cosmetic detail which Lincoln had ignored as a bachelor, but she also provided him with a synopsis of newspaper articles which were relevant to his career. Additionally, she wrote letters during his political campaigns and played hostess at social events. People who knew them in Springfield felt that they were a loving couple and indulgent parents to a household of what would grow to accommodate four sons.

Lincoln's Political Career Advances

During his 1846 election campaign, Lincoln did not make the U.S. entry into the Mexican American War an issue, an omission which likely helped him to win by a significant majority. However, once in office he disputed President James Polk's stance that Mexico, by attacking American soldiers on American soil, had initiated the war. He accused Polk of leading the country into war by misrepresentation, a risky move against a popular president, particularly for a congressman representing a state that had supported the war.

Lincoln left his political career behind after the term ended and practiced law in Springfield. His career as a lawyer was a successful one with many clients. It seemed that he had left behind him the hardscrabble poverty of his childhood: he was well known, respected, even liked. His failed run for the Senate in 1854 led him to give up on the Whig Party, which was in its final days, to join a new political party which had many former Whigs in its membership. The Republicans were adamantly opposed to slavery, the divisive issue in 19th century America. The anti-slavery platform of the Republican Party called for Kansas to be admitted to the Union as a free state, halting the extension of slavery in the west as new states joined the Union, and the repeal of the Kansas-Nebraska Act. The negotiator spirit which had held the nation together with the political glue of compromise was failing as the country began to realize that it would have to grapple with slavery regardless of the consequences.

The Lincoln-Douglas Debates

Although Democrat James Buchanan won the 1856 presidential election, the Republican Party won 30 percent of the Illinois popular vote and the majority of the state's northern counties. Two years later, Lincoln was the Republican candidate for U.S. senator from Illinois. What followed—a series of seven debates between the Republican candidate Lincoln and his Democratic opponent Stephen A. Douglas—is regarded as one of the most significant political competitions in American history.

Douglas had already made a name for himself as a national figure based on his involvement in the Compromise of 1850. Lincoln was known in Illinois, but lacked Douglas' influence. It seemed like an unequal match-up, not only in prominence—Douglas was known as the Democratic Party's "Little Giant" for his oratory—but also visually. Douglas was diminutive in height, Lincoln towering. But Douglas did enter the fray with a significant disadvantage: his opposition to the admission of Kansas as a slave state infuriated southern Democrats. Clearly, slavery was a litmus test for the candidates.

Lincoln didn't falter. The delivery of his "House Divided" speech alerted the audience that the United States had to decide whether it would be a nation which allowed slavery or opposed it; there could no longer be a middle ground where half the nation supported slavery and the other half opposed it. Lincoln viewed slavery as a moral issue. Douglas did not. He supported the view that the decision was not for the federal government to make, but for the local legislatures. Abolitionists were commonly regarded as radicals, and Douglas freely applied the term to his opponent, knowing that racial views in the United States were not devoid of bigotry.

Ultimately, Douglas won the election for the Senate, but Lincoln had made a name for himself on an issue which would dominate the next presidential election.

Chapter Three

The Election of 1860

"I therefore consider that in the view of the Constitution and the laws, the Union is unbroken; and to the extent of my ability I shall take care as the Constitution itself expressly enjoins upon me that the laws of the Union be faithfully executed in all the states."

—Abraham Lincoln

Lincoln's defeat in the election for Senate had not placed him on the political sidelines. For the next 16 months he traveled across the North, campaigning for Republican candidates, endorsing the abolitionist cause with eloquent oratory rather than the bombastic rhetoric of most speakers during that time. He was also building up a network of support for his own future candidacy; a shrewd politician, Lincoln knew that as a new name in national politics, his loyalty to other party members would build him a foundation of experienced political veterans who would be useful in his ambitions. His stance on slavery was well known and was a rallying cry for abolitionists. At the 1856 Republican Party convention, when asked for his thoughts on the threat of secession by the Southern states, Lincoln had answered: "We say to the Southern disunionists, we won't go out of the Union, and you shan't."

Lincoln for President

The election of 1860, because of the looming split between South and North which teetered on the issue of which candidate would be elected, was perhaps the most important one in American history. It was also the most bizarre, with four candidates vying for the office of president. Meeting in Charleston, South Carolina, the Democrats supported Stephen Douglas as the person most likely to defeat the Republican nominee. But southern Democrats, distrusting him because he believed that new territories entering the union should be allowed to decide for themselves whether or not slavery should be permitted in their region, walked out of the convention to hold their own, where they nominated John C. Breckenridge. The Constitutional Union Party nominated John Bell, a slave-owning Southerner as their candidate, believing that it was better to avoid taking a stand on the issue of slavery. Bell reflected their duality: he supported slavery but was against extending it into the newly added territories.

The Republicans met in Chicago knowing that they had an excellent chance to win the White House with the right candidate, someone who could carry the Northern states, particularly Illinois, Indiana, Pennsylvania, and New Jersey. Senator William Seward of New York was a vocal advocate for the abolition of slavery and was convinced that he was the popular candidate. But the party leaders, doubting that Seward could carry Indiana and Pennsylvania, supported the Stop Seward movement. Although Lincoln had instructed his campaign managers not to make any political deals, zealous Lincoln supporters promised that, if Lincoln won, he would offer cabinet posts to prominent citizens of Pennsylvania and Indiana. On the third ballot, Lincoln had the votes he needed.

Campaigning was not part of presidential tradition in the mid-nineteenth century and only Douglas went out to give speeches to the public, where he was consistently asked what would happen if Lincoln were elected. Pro-slavery Southerners who spoke on the campaign trail warned that if Lincoln were elected, the Southern states would secede. Lincoln's campaign supporters were enthusiastic about their frontier-born, rail-splitting candidate, holding rallies, barbecues, and marches to promote Lincoln. Lincoln's opponents mocked the ungainly, self-educated Republican candidate and predicted that, if he were elected president, his term in office would hold the United States up to ridicule in front of the world. It was a time when there were comparatively few rules restricting reporters in their coverage, and the cartoons and articles exploited the racial bias of the era. One Southerner predicted that Lincoln's plan as president would mean that, within a decade, Southern white children would be enslaved by their former slaves. Lincoln was not on the ballot in the Southern states.

Journalists who discussed with Lincoln the South's threat to secede if he were elected found him doubtful that they would follow through. He told an Indiana delegation that the Union must be preserved. He impressed his audience with his certainty, and also with a sense that he would be able to meet whatever challenge arose. But Lincoln and the North may have failed to realize the deep roots of Southern grievances. The South felt that the North was unjustly imposing its abolitionist fervor on the states where slavery was legal and this, in Southern eyes, violated the Constitution.

Lincoln Wins the Election

A Lincoln victory would also introduce a pivotal change in a nation which, since its birth, had been politically dominated by the South: no Northern president had ever been re-elected to the office; southerners had been the Speakers of the House of Representatives; the majority of the justices on the Supreme Court had been Southerners. As a Western candidate, Lincoln brought a new political energy into the election process, but he also heralded the unknown for a nation whose power elite had been firmly rooted in tradition, and perhaps entitlement, for a long time.

The election gave Lincoln the victory in all the Northern states but one, Delaware. His margin of victory was narrow; he only received 180 electoral votes, but it was enough. When he learned the news of his victory, Lincoln is said to have hurried home from the telegraph office to announce, "Mary, we are elected!"

The newspapers reflected the philosophical viewpoints of their readership when they reported on the election results. The *Richmond Dispatch* wrote: "The event is the most deplorable one that has happened in the history of the country. The Union may be preserved in spite of it. We think it will; but we are prepared to expect trouble. We have already one sign from South Carolina, and this may be followed by others of a more serious character."

The Daily Spy of Worcester, Massachusetts described Lincoln's victory as "the first triumph of a great political revolution. . . . It is not only regular and lawful, but is necessary to restore the old spirit and policy of the country, and give peace to the land. It comes hard for those Southern extremists to be driven from power . . . but they will submit to necessity and become less dangerous, for the sentiment of the Southern people will constrain them to good behavior."

The *Courier* of New Orleans began its coverage with the headline

THE CRISIS: "The election of Abraham Lincoln to the chief magistracy of the country by the . . . fanatics and negrophilists who have been flocking to his standards . . . has awakened throughout the South a spirit of stubborn resistance which it will be found is impossible to quell."

Lame duck President James Buchanan, whose term in office had done nothing to address the simmering problem of slavery and the South, did not believe that secession was legal. However, he also believed that using military force to keep the South in the Union was a violation of the Constitution. There would be no direction from the White House in the intervening months before Lincoln took office.

Lincoln's Trip to His Inauguration

Lincoln left Springfield, Illinois for Washington D.C. on February 11, 1861. He told the crowd that gathered at the train station that he owed everything to Springfield and its people, and that he was leaving with a task resting upon him which was greater than what George Washington had faced. To the crowd which met him when his train stopped in Lafayette, Indiana, he insisted that while Americans differed in their political opinions, they were all united in their feeling for the Union, and all believed in what he called "the maintenance of the Union, of every star and every stripe of the glorious flag." Speaking at a reception hosted by the German Industrial Association in Cincinnati, Ohio, Lincoln declined to express what course he would follow regarding the "national difficulties" until the last moment. When he arrived in Pittsburgh, he was astonished by the size of the crowds who had come out to meet him. "I could not help thinking, my friends, as I traveled in the rain through your crowded streets, on my way here, that if all that people were in favor of the Union, it can certainly be in no great danger – it will be preserved."

The crowds in Ashtabula, Ohio, called for Mary Todd Lincoln to appear, but Lincoln replied that he doubted that she would do so, and he had always found it very difficult to make her do what she did not want to. Upon his arrival in Westfield, New York, he asked to meet 12-year old Grace Bedell, the girl who had written to him earlier to suggest that he should grow a beard, which he had done. Grace was present and received kisses from the president-elect who had adopted the look she had suggested. Walt Whitman, writing of his first sight of Abraham Lincoln when the president-elect appeared in New York City, wrote, "I had, I say, a capital view of . . . Mr. Lincoln: his looks and gait; his perfect composure and coolness; his unusual and uncouth height; his dress of complete black, stovepipe hat pushed back on his head; dark-brown complexion; seamed and wrinkled yet canny-looking face; black, bush head of hair; disproportionately long neck; and his hands held behind, as he stood observing the people."

New York was not all politics; Mary Todd Lincoln and her children visited P.T. Barnum's museum and in the evening, Lincoln went to the Academy of Music to see a new opera by Verdi; he was serenaded with *The Star Spangled Banner* by the audience. But in Philadelphia, he received a letter from Senator William Seward alerting him that there was a plot to assassinate him in Baltimore. Detective Allen Pinkerton accompanied Lincoln to Baltimore, where the telegraph lines out of the city were cut so that news of Lincoln's trip would not spread. Pinkerton, convinced that the threat was a serious one, convinced Lincoln that he should enter the nation's capital covertly, changing his itinerary. Lincoln didn't like the suggestion but followed Pinkerton's advice, donning a soft felt hat instead of his well-known stovepipe, hunching to reduce his height, and draping his overcoat over his shoulders. Arriving in Baltimore in the middle of the night, they got on a different train and reached Washington D.C. at 6:00 a.m.

The press was contemptuous of his stealthy arrival to the city where he would take office and the story spread that in order to protect himself, Lincoln had dressed as a woman. He had not, but in retrospect Lincoln regretted what he had done. It was an inauspicious start to his presidency, but circumstances were already working against his office.

By the time Lincoln was inaugurated in 1861, the Confederate States of America, consisting then of seven southern states, was a new nation. South Carolina seceded before the end of the year; by February 1, 1861, Texas, Louisiana, Mississippi, Georgia, Alabama and Florida had seceded as well. Long-time American statesman Jefferson Davis was elected president of the Confederacy.

As the North waited to see what would happen next, the South was busy building a nation.

Chapter Four

The House Divides

*"Much is said of peace and no man desires peace more
ardently than I. Still I am yet unprepared to give up the
Union for a peace which, so achieved, could not be of much
duration."*

—Abraham Lincoln

Much has been said and written of the men Lincoln chose
to serve in his Cabinet when he became president. In her
prize-winning book, author Doris Kearns Goodwin
describes the *Team of Rivals* he chose to advise him as a
"spirited but often undisciplined set of horses which
President Lincoln was expected to give rein to and rein in
as well." Lincoln had actually settled on the men he wanted
to serve in his Cabinet on the day after the election, and the
final result was nearly the same as he had originally
intended.

His political rival William Seward was Secretary of
State; Salmon P. Chase was Secretary of the Treasury;
Secretary of War Simon Cameron was replaced by Edwin
M. Stanton in 1862; and Edward Bates was Attorney
General. They were all lawyers, eager for power, strong-
minded, well-educated and aware that their educations were
superior to that of the president they would serve. They
started out that service by thinking Lincoln a man of
inferior abilities, especially in comparison to their own. In

assembling his Cabinet, Lincoln demonstrated what they would all eventually learn: that he was a shrewd and flexible politician, a discerning judge of character, and a man of empathy who understood the fears of the electorate better than more experienced politicians. Indicative of Lincoln's style of decision-making was his ability to listen to the opinions of others. However, he made his own decisions, not depending upon others to decide for him.

The War Begins

Lincoln's presidency had a short honeymoon. His plan to resupply Fort Sumter, which was located in South Carolina's Charleston Harbor, and the site of the first state to secede from the Union, was met with a military response as Confederate forces bombarded the fort beginning on April 12, 1861. Major Robert Anderson, who was in command of Fort Sumter, refused to surrender. By the next day, Confederate cannon fire had penetrated the fort's brick walls. Out of ammunition, Anderson had no choice but to surrender.

Lincoln's call for 75,000 Union volunteers in response to the Southern rebellion led the states of Tennessee, North Carolina, and Virginia to join their sister states as part of the Confederacy. Lincoln offered command of the Union troops to General Robert E. Lee but Lee, a Virginian, declined and resigned his commission in the United States Army. He accepted the offer to command the military and naval forces of the Confederacy, his ties to his home state overpowering his bond with the Union.

The war began badly for the North when the Confederate Army defeated General Irvin McDowell's

Union forces at the First Battle of Bull Run. Washington D.C. residents came out to watch the battle as if it were entertainment but were dismayed when the reality of battle made them vulnerable. Although the Union Army had 35,000 troops, and the Confederates only 20,000, the Southern forces were able to force the Yankees to retreat back to Washington D.C. The results of the battle stunned the North, which had expected the war to end quickly.

Lincoln turned to George B. McClellan, who had graduated second in his West Point class, to replace McDowell, and named him Commander of the Army of the Potomac. McClellan was a superb organizer who drilled the green recruits who had enlisted, teaching them to be soldiers and earning their affection and loyalty in return. He was in command of the largest military force which the United States assembled up to that time. McClellan was as impressed with his own abilities as he was dismissive of the Commander-in-Chief, describing Lincoln as a gorilla and a baboon who was unworthy of his office. At one point, when Lincoln went to McClellan's home to meet with the general, McClellan kept him waiting for half an hour and then sent word that he had gone to bed and could not meet with Lincoln. He prepared a defense of Washington D. C. to protect it from the threat of Confederate attack, but McClellan consistently overestimated the size of the Confederate forces against him and was disinclined to meet the enemy in battle. His excessive caution so frustrated Lincoln that the president said, "If General McClellan is not using the Army, I should like to borrow it for a time."

On those occasions when McClellan actually did engage in battle, if defeated, he blamed the president, the

War Department and the Secretary of Defense for the loss. The Battle of Antietam in 1862 was a victory, albeit a costly one with a horrific loss of men, but McClellan failed to pursue Lee's forces, and Lincoln removed him as the commander of the Army of the Potomac.

Antietam was a frustrating and tragic victory for the Union. After twelve hours of fighting, the battle lines had only shifted one hundred yards, but 23,000 soldiers were killed or wounded across that distance. But Antietam, despite McClellan's failure to capitalize on his achievement, did provide Lincoln with enough of a victory to make a political announcement which would give the war a moral compass.

Emancipation Proclamation

The war needed a cause for the Union, and on January 1, 1863, Lincoln provided one when he issued the final Emancipation Proclamation, which freed all slaves in the territories which were controlled by the Confederacy. At the start of the war, Lincoln realized that abolition was not a strong enough justification for war, as the Constitution permitted slavery in the United States. But the war changed the nature of slavery. The slaves who assisted their Confederate masters by cooking, digging trenches, and aiding the soldiers were now part of the war effort, and Lincoln could use his powers as Commander-in-Chief to identify slavery as a Confederate tool that harmed Union forces. When his Cabinet learned, in July of 1862, that Lincoln planned to issue the Proclamation, it was William Seward who urged him to wait for a military victory to make the announcement, because if he did so after a Union defeat, the proclamation would seem to be an act of desperation rather than one of conviction and strength. Lincoln did so, and began 1863 with the Emancipation Proclamation, which freed the slaves in the states which were rebelling against the Union.

The Emancipation Proclamation had an international effect as well as a domestic one. France and Great Britain had leaned toward supporting the Confederacy, but in general, Europeans opposed slavery. When Lincoln altered the course of the Civil War from an effort to preserve the Union to one intending to abolish slavery, European nations were disinclined to intervene on behalf of the South. The South had been counting on European endorsement, and this decision was a major political blow to their war plans.

The Emancipation Proclamation also transformed the role of African-Americans in the conflict by allowing them to serve in the military. Within five months, General Order No. 143 had established the United States Colored Troops, and when the war ended in 1865, more than 200,000 African-American troops had served their country.

For Lincoln, who personally regarded slavery as morally wrong but had not been willing to make it a political crusade, the Emancipation Proclamation was the cornerstone of his presidential legacy. "I never, in my life," he said, "felt more certain that I was doing right than I do in signing this paper. If my name ever goes into history it will be for this act, and my whole soul is in it."

The Union had a cause worth fighting for, but still lacked a commanding general who could win. By June of 1863, General George Meade was the fifth man to command the Army of the Potomac in less than a year. But in the west, the prognosis was somewhat brighter. General Ulysses S. Grant had impressed Lincoln as a general who was willing to fight and he was given command of the Army of the West with instructions to capture Vicksburg on the Mississippi River. Doing so would sever the Confederacy in half and take control of the Mississippi River. Grant was a dogged, persistent officer, but Vicksburg would be a challenge; moreover, there were politicians in Washington D.C. who were calling for Grant's removal. One newspaper descried Grant as foolish, drunken and stupid, a man who could not organize or fight. Lincoln's reply to Grant's detractors: "Grant advises me that he will take Vicksburg by the Fourth of July, and I believe he will do it; and he shall have the chance."

Gettysburg

The war would continue for nearly two more years, but the momentum had shifted. It was, after all, a glorious Fourth of July for the Union. Lincoln also learned that his faith in General Grant had been justified: Vicksburg had fallen. When Lincoln received the news from Grant of Vicksburg's surrender, he said, "Thank God. The Father of Waters again goes unvexed to the sea."

In November of that year, Lincoln spoke at the dedication of the Gettysburg Cemetery. His short speech was not, as legend claims, written spontaneously on the back of an envelope. The Gettysburg Address, for all its brevity, was an eloquent eulogy to the sacrifices made by the soldiers who died in battle, but it was also a reminder that a grateful nation had an obligation to honor their sacrifice with a renewed dedication to freedom. Lincoln, who cherished the United States for its democratic principles, told his audience that "we here highly resolve these dead shall not have died in vain; that the nation shall have a new birth of freedom, and that government of the people, by the people, for the people, shall not perish from the earth."

Chapter Five

The Tide Turns

"With malice toward none; with charity for all; with firmness in the right, as God gives us to see the right, let us strive on to finish the work we are in; to bind up the nation's wounds; to care for him who shall have borne the battle, and for his widow, and his orphan."

—Abraham Lincoln

With Vicksburg conquered in the West and Gettysburg a crushing defeat for Lee's Army, the fortunes of war were turning in favor of the Union, but not fast enough. The Union needed more troops but the North was weary of war. When Congress conscripted all men between the ages of 20 to 45 for military service rioting broke out across the nation, with the most serious violence in New York City. Troops who had fought in Gettysburg were called to restore order to the city and instead of battling Southerners, they found themselves subduing rioters. The mob set government buildings to flame; an orphan asylum for African-Americans was razed; the homes of African-Americans were ransacked. The rioters may have targeted innocent African-Americans for their vengeance, but the actual object of their ire was a provision in the conscription law that a man could avoid the draft by paying three hundred dollars. The average man, many of whom were Irish immigrants struggling for economic survival, could never have raised that kind of money. It was a loophole for the rich.

The Election of 1864

Although Union victories at Vicksburg and Gettysburg had seriously damaged the South's ability to achieve its aims of independence, the Confederates refused to surrender. If Lincoln were defeated in the upcoming 1864 election, their leaders reasoned, there was a chance that his successor would end the war and accept the independence of the Southern states. George McClellan, running on the Democratic ticket, was Lincoln's opponent for the office of president; however, even within the Republican Party Lincoln had serious competition in his bid to be the nominee. Cabinet Secretary Salmon P. Chase was one of those challengers, supported by other Republicans who believed that Lincoln was not aggressive enough in ending slavery. Abolitionists Frederick Douglass and Elizabeth Cady Stanton, a supporter of women's suffrage, formed a political party, Radical Democracy, with General John C. Fremont as their candidate.

As the South expected, the strongest challenge to Lincoln came from McClellan. The Democrats' party platform included plans to end the war and come to terms with the Confederacy after what they regarded as four years of failure to restore the Union by force. They opposed the military draft, emancipation of the slaves, and what they termed Lincoln's violation of civil liberties. The candidate, despite his antipathy to Lincoln, did not endorse the party's stand on ending the war because he felt that his comrades-in-arms could not have fought in vain.

The Republicans made a few changes to enhance their chances of victory in 1864; the former vice president Hannibal Hamlin was rejected in favor of pro-Union Tennessee governor Andrew Johnson. The Party endorsed a constitutional amendment banning slavery. It agreed to insist on unconditional surrender from the Confederacy.

Lincoln nonetheless felt that his re-election prospects were futile. He had his Cabinet secretly sign a pledge promising to cooperate with the new president-elect so that the Union would be saved before the inauguration. He explained to a visitor to the White house, "I am going to be beaten . . . and unless some great change takes place, badly beaten."

Mary Todd Lincoln

His re-election was not only important to him. His wife, Mary Todd Lincoln, needed Abraham Lincoln to be re-elected. Mary had always loved fine clothing and as the First Lady, she felt that she should uphold a fashionable image. Her shopping attracted press attention at a time when the nation felt that extravagance was a sign of disregard for the hardships of war.

She had also spent funds on refurbishing the White House, which had been neglected during the recent presidential administrations; although replacing worn-out wallpaper and broken furniture might have been necessary, the timing was not right. The fact that she overspent the budget by $6,000 did not help her cause.

In terms of temperament, her public rages inspired Lincoln's secretary John Hay to term her "the hellcat." On one occasion, she became jealous when she saw a military officer's wife riding beside the president as he reviewed the troops, and she unleashed her temper on the woman, leaving her in tears. Julia Grant, wife of Lieutenant General Ulysses S. Grant, was present at the scene, and was determined that she would never spend an evening with Mrs. Lincoln - which is why, when an invitation to attend Ford's Theatre on April 14, 1865 was extended to the Grants, the invitation was declined.

Some of Mary Lincoln's problems were of her own making. But she suffered greatly during the White House years. The Lincolns' 11-year-old son Willie died in 1862 of typhoid fever; her youngest half-brother, an officer in the Confederate Army, died in battle. As a way of dealing with her grief, Mary would hold séances in the White House at a time when spiritualism was popular. According to Mary, Willie's spirit came to her accompanied by her brother's spirit.

It was Mary Todd Lincoln's tragic fate that her political aspirations for her husband would culminate in the presidency at a time when her Southern birth would mark her as a woman of suspected loyalties by the North, and as a traitor to her homeland by the South. As a Westerner, she was looked down by Washington D.C.'s social elite; the west was regarded as rustic and unpolished.

By 1864, Mary's unpaid shopping bills were coming home to roost and she needed money. She accepted money from political favor-seekers who asked her to speak in support of their requests. Her wild spending continued. In four months, she ordered 300 pairs of gloves. If Lincoln lost his bid for re-election, Mary confessed to her seamstress, "I do not know what would become of us all.

To me, to him, there is more at stake in this election than he dreams of."

There was fear that the First Lady's spending would turn into a campaign issue which the Democrats would exploit. Mary excused her spending on the grounds that in order to represent her husband's presidency with dignity and respect, she had to overcome the preconceived notions of their western background.

But in September, the Lincolns' fears that he would be defeated in his re-election bid were put to rest. General William T. Sherman telegraphed the president: "Atlanta is ours, and fairly won."

With the fall of Atlanta, the Democratic hopes of a victory faded. Lincoln won the election with 212 out of 233 electoral votes and carried all but three states. As 1864 came to a close, he could anticipate his second term in office, when following the Union victory and the end of the war, he planned to implement his plans to bring the South back into the Union.

After the years of travail, Lincoln had surely earned the time to savor victory and peace. But his election to a second term as president would be his death sentence.

Chapter Six

The End

"Now he belongs to the ages."

—Edwin M. Stanton

The years when Robert E. Lee had seemed invincible were over. In the final days of the war, as Lee was attempting to avoid surrender by meeting up with Confederate forces in the west, Grant had already discussed the proposed terms of surrender with Lincoln, who did not want to inflict humiliation on the defeated South. Soldiers would have to surrender their rifles, but they could keep their mules. Lincoln wanted to restore the Confederacy to its status as part of the Union, not to give the Rebels cause to continue to fight. His terms were generous; the soldiers were even to be given food, because the Confederate Army had not been well supplied in its final days of combat.

General Grant sent letters urging Lee to avoid further bloodshed. Lee refused to concede that his cause was lost, but he concurred with Grant in the wish to avoid the shedding of more bloodshed with the accompanying loss of life and destruction of property. The generals met at the home of Wilmer McLean in Appomattox, Virginia on April 9, 1865. Lee was dressed in full regalia; his uniform was new and clean, his sword jeweled, his bearing as dignified as if he came as victor. Grant, on the other hand, did not bring his sword with him. His boots and clothes were spattered with mud. The two men reminisced about their service in Mexico in a war where Southerners and Northerners had fought together, on the same side. Grant wrote out the terms of surrender and Lee accepted them in writing.

April 14, 1865

The war was over. The North was jubilant. On April 14, 1865, General Robert Anderson, whose surrender of Fort Sumter to Confederate forces in 1861 had been the prelude to four long years of death and suffering, returned to the site of that early defeat. The flag of Fort Sumter was raised over the fort. It was a symbolic gesture, but a powerful one.

At the White House that day, the Lincolns were enjoying breakfast together. Their oldest son Robert, who had finally gotten his wish to enlist in the army despite his mother's objections, had been present at the surrender at McLean House. Mary Lincoln discussed plans for attending the theatre that night; she wanted to see *Our American Cousin* at Ford's Theatre and hoped that General and Mrs. Grant would join them.

Returning to work, Lincoln met with the Speaker of the House to discuss his plans for the reconstruction of the South. He also met with John P. Hale, who had been appointed the minister to Spain; Hale's daughter Lucy was secretly engaged to an actor, a member of the famed Booth thespian clan. The couple had been seen in public, but their engagement had not been officially announced. Her parents disapproved of the bond and hoped that the move to Spain would end the relationship. John Wilkes Booth had wooed Lucy with fervor but the couple had been quarrelling lately and Booth had been stricken with jealousy when he saw her dancing with the President's son, Robert Lincoln.

After meeting with Hale, Lincoln met with the members of his Cabinet to discuss plans for Southern reconstruction. His Cabinet ministers agreed with Lincoln that a punitive reconstruction would not benefit the South or the North economically. General Grant, who was at the meeting of the Cabinet, informed Lincoln that he and his wife would not be able to join the President and his own wife at the theatre because they were taking a train that night for a visit with their children. Edwin Stanton, who had also been invited, later decided not to go.

Lincoln continued to work, signing a pardon for a young soldier who had deserted his post. Lincoln made the comment that the young man could do more good above the ground than under it. He spoke with a former slave whose husband had served in the Union army but hadn't received all his pay checks, and Lincoln told her that he would investigate the matter. There was other business to attend to before he returned to have dinner with his family and dress for the evening at the theatre.

The Lincolns arrived late at Ford's Theatre and the play had already begun. When the Lincolns arrived, the play stopped as the orchestra played *Hail to the Chief*, and then the play continued. When the intermission came, Lincoln's bodyguard left his post outside the box to go to the nearby saloon to get a drink. He didn't return.

Mary Lincoln was in an affectionate mood, sitting close to her husband, holding his hand. Act Three of the play was underway. At some point after 10:15 p.m., John Wilkes Booth entered the box and shot the President in the back of the head. The point of entry of the bullet was approximately three inches behind the left ear; the bullet would travel over seven inches into the brain. Booth shouted something, but accounts differ on whether his words were "Freedom" or "Sic Semper Tyrannis." He then leaped to the stage and ran out of the theatre.

Dr. Charles Leale was the first of a series of doctors who would tend to the president. Dr. Leale, examining the wound, saw that it was mortal. Lincoln was moved across the street to the Peterson House. As the vigil began, Washington D.C.'s most well-known doctors came by to try to do what they could, but the president continued to weaken, his breathing fading. Learning of the shooting, a crowd gathered outside the Peterson House. On April 15 at 7:22 a.m., nine hours after he had been shot, Lincoln died.

The Nation Grieves

In Washington D.C., flags were lowered to half-staff and church bells began to toll. Offices and stores closed. Rain fell and the wind blew as Nature joined the mourners in grieving for the fallen president.

The procession, which lasted over two hours, was led by African-American soldiers, the Twenty-Second United States Colored Infantry. Civilians, soldiers, government workers and elected officials paid their respects to the man whose perseverance and fortitude had brought the nation to victory. Lincoln's body travelled by train back home to Springfield; all along the way, Americans came out as the train passed through their towns. On May 4, Lincoln returned to Springfield, Illinois.

Speaking at the graveside, Bishop Simpson said, "Hushed is thy voice, but its echoes of liberty are ringing through the world and the sons of bondage listen with joy. We crown thee as our martyr—and humanity enthrones thee as her triumphant son. Hero, Martyr, Friend, Farewell."

Chapter Seven

The Legacy of Lincoln

"We say we are for the Union. . . We . . . hold the power, and bear the responsibility. In giving freedom to the slave, we assure freedom to the free–honorable alike in what we give, and what we preserve. We shall nobly save, or meanly lose, the last best hope of earth."

—Abraham Lincoln

Although the Civil War dominated Abraham Lincoln's presidency, it was not the only subject which received his attention. Presidents, in good times and bad, must multitask, and that was true of Lincoln as well. The passing of the Homestead Act in 1862 offered 160 acres of free land to people who were willing to travel west to settle. The country's state university system was established by the Morrill Act of 1862. The Department of Agriculture was added to the government. Thanksgiving, the day of celebration when Americans honored their Pilgrim forefathers, was instituted as a national holiday.

But he will always be remembered as the president who fought to save the Union, engaging his nation in a bitter and unpopular struggle to preserve what he regarded as his duty as the leader of the United States. He was resolute in his endurance, despite the fact that the battlefields of the war were soaked in blood. He took no pleasure in war, but from his point of view, the South left him no choice when the states began to tear asunder what Lincoln felt must remain whole. He was a pragmatic politician, not an idealist, but he believed in the ideals of the country's founding.

For most of his presidency, he was second-guessed and insulted, in speech and in print, by leaders who regarded him as ill-suited to occupy the office that Washington, Jefferson and Jackson had been elected to as well. However, in 1982 the *Chicago Tribune* charged forty-nine historians and political scientists to rate all the American presidents up to that time based on their qualities of leadership, their ability to manage crises, their political skills, appointments and character. Abraham Lincoln, the frontiersman who was born in poverty and had minimal formal education, was placed at the top of the list in every category.

To his detractors, Abraham Lincoln transformed the presidency in ways that suborned the rights of the states, trampling on civil liberties in his zeal to preserve the Union. His advocates supported the strength of his dedication to the preservation of the Union, reverence for democracy, and the abolition of slavery. Had he failed in any of these ideals, the United States would have evolved into a very different entity from what history has seen.

No one, not the most learned historian or the most experienced politician, can estimate how Lincoln would view the United States as it is now, 151 years after his death. But that it still stands, slavery abolished and freedom cherished, validates his efforts.